VIKING
SOCIAL MARKETING

I0056754

Copyright © All rights reserved.

ABOUT YOUR RIGHTS: This eBook is intended for your personal use only. It does not include any other rights.

IMPORTANT LEGAL DISCLAIMER: This book is protected by international copyright law and may not be copied, reproduced, given away, or used to create derivative works without the publisher's expressed permission. The publisher retains full copyrights to this book.

The author has made every reasonable effort to be as accurate and complete as possible in the creation of this book and to ensure that the information provided is free from errors; however, the author/publisher/ reseller assumes no responsibility for errors, omissions, or contrary interpretation of the subject matter herein and does not warrant or represent at any time that the contents within are accurate due to the rapidly changing nature of the Internet.

Any perceived slights of specific persons, peoples, or organizations are unintentional.

The purpose of this book is to educate and there are no guarantees of income, sales or results implied. The publisher/author/reseller/distributor can therefore not be held accountable for any poor results you may attain when implementing the techniques or when following any guidelines set out for you in this book.

Any product, website, and company names mentioned in this report are the trademarks or copyright properties of their respective owners. The author/publisher/reseller/distributor are not associated or affiliated with them in any way. Nor does the referred product, website, and company names sponsor, endorse, or approve this product.

AFFILIATE/COMPENSATION DISCLAIMER: Unless otherwise expressly stated, you should assume that the links contained in this book may be affiliate links and either the author/publisher/reseller/distributor will earn commission if you click on them and buy the product/service mentioned in this book. However, the author/publisher/reseller/distributor disclaim any liability that may result from your involvement with any such websites/products. You should thoroughly research before buying mentioned products or services.

This constitutes the entire license agreement. Any disputes or terms not discussed in this agreement are at the sole discretion of the publisher.

Viking Social Marketing Page

Chapter 1:
Intro to Social Marketing

Social media marketing has come a long way in the last several years and has changed the way many businesses think about marketing in general. For some marketers, social followers have replaced email addresses, posts and tweets have replaced promotional emails, and likes have replaced email opens. Virtually every successful business today has not only a social media presence, but a clearly defined social media strategy.

Most of these strategies revolve around posting consistent content. But it's more than just posting promotions and offers. A successful social strategy will include various types of nonpromotional content for various types of goals. Posting about a charitable cause associates your brand with feelings of goodwill. Posting about trendy topics makes your brand seem relevant. Posting useful tips without a sales pitch makes your business come off as genuinely helpful. Posting humorous or "feel-good" content associates your business with positive emotions, and so on. But more importantly, these types of non-promotional posts are accomplishing two other goals. First, they're encouraging social sharing, which grows your following even more. Secondly, they're creating top-of-mind awareness for your brand. People will get used to seeing your content and your business name, logo, and USP. As a result, when they have a problem that your business fixes, they'll be more likely to think of you first.

All of those social media concepts revolve around organic activity. However, the major social media platforms today have also developed robust paid advertising systems. The most game-changing of these has been the concept of social "native advertising". Native advertising refers to advertisements that have the appearance of organic content with the exception of a tiny one-word disclaimer somewhere designating it as "sponsored" or an "advertisement". This new form of paid social media advertising has proven to be remarkably effective because social media consumers are already in the habit of looking at, consuming, and engaging with anything that looks like an organic post in their social feeds. In addition to this, the line between organic posts and paid native ads have become increasingly blurred as these native ads act and function just like organic content (they can be shared, liked, etc.) and businesses now have the ability to pay to promote an organic post to give it further reach.

Now that we've discussed social marketing in general, let's have a closer look at each of the top social media platforms in more detail.

Facebook

One could argue that there has truly never been anything like Facebook. The undeniable king of social networks took the web by storm several years ago and has since become a household name. Almost everyone has a Facebook account (and about 3/4 of all U.S. adults check it regularly). There is simply no other platform so consistently and universally used all around the globe.

For many businesses and organizations, their Facebook presence has replaced their actual website (at least in importance) because people are more likely to interact and receive updates there. Is there a blackout in your city or an emergency in your local area? There's a good chance the power company or news agencies will be posting updates on Facebook more quickly and consistently than their own websites. Why? Because that's where everybody is. And you need to be where your audience is.

Facebook has done an excellent job of developing an environment where people stay inside the platform. Although links to the outside are easy to create, it's now just as easy and perhaps more beneficial to keep things inside Facebook. For example, until a couple years ago, most people who wanted to share videos did so by linking to a Youtube video.

Today, however, Facebook has made it both quick and easy to upload videos within the platform and has even made it the best option by allowing Facebook videos to autoplay as people are scrolling through their newsfeeds, making this option the most beneficial for people doing the sharing and the most pleasing for those doing the consuming. The result? After years of this sort of structuring and positioning, Facebook users now actually feel more comfortable when they remain inside Facebook. People trust and feel safe with the Facebook interface and prefer to consume content inside of it. Hence the enormous success of Facebook Native Ads.

The point is, if you want to market your business or brand in the place where your audience spends most of their time and in a context in which they feel most comfortable (hint: you do), then you need to be marketing on Facebook.

To fully get the point across, here are some for statistics that'll give you a fuller appreciation of Facebook's size, reach, and importance. Almost 40% of the entire world's online population is on Facebook. Of the remainder who do not use Facebook, half of them live with someone who does. There are currently almost 1.8 billion monthly active users and that's growing by 500,000 new users per day. Almost 1.2 billion daily logins occur and 6 new profiles are created every second. More than 1,000,000 hours of video viewing time takes place on Facebook. Over 250 Billion images have been uploaded, which boils down to about 350,000,000 per day.

And just in case you were wondering about the level of engagement, Facebook users generate 4 million Likes, 510,000 comments, and 293,000 status updates... per minute. With a growing and engaged user base like that, it's no wonder more than 40% of marketers report that Facebook is a critical part of their business. The question is, how do you make it work for you?

Paid Vs Organic Marketing

A quick note on paid vs organic Facebook marketing. Ideally, a solid Facebook marketing strategy should include a mix of both of these. Organic marketing is an excellent and critical way to provide content and value, keep your audience engaged, gain brand exposure, grow loyal followers, and establish rapport. Paid ads are a great way to boost those efforts as well as to accomplish a variety of "off-facebook" goals such as website visitors, lead generation, and sales. Facebook's masterfully established "native" ad style has made paid ads even more effective than anyone could have imagined.

Twitter

Twitter is an incredibly powerful online news and social networking service. It's in a unique league of it's own due to several features that set it apart from other social networking platforms like Facebook, LinkedIn, and GooglePlus.

Firstly, one of the main functions and uses of Twitter is as a news/events broadcasting channel. In many ways it's more like a news ticker than a social networking platform (albeit a news ticker where you get to choose what news you want to hear about by choosing who you follow). In fact, it's become a must-have resource for news networks and journalists who want to stay in the know about anything newsworthy in their areas. Journalists make up almost 25% of all verified Twitter accounts.

Secondly, Twitter is all about short burst broadcasts. All posts consist of tiny bite sized messages, called Tweets, of 140 characters or less, or some combination of video/images and text. Users can broadcast and receive these messages via SMS, Mobile App, and the Twitter website interface.

Interaction with these posts can take the form of replies, likes, and retweets, with the latter being the ultimate sign of a successful tweet. For businesses and organizations, Twitter is used not only as a place to network and broadcast news, but also as a way to keep audiences updated about content published elsewhere. For example, some businesses primarily use Twitter as the "hey look" step in their content marketing plan, in which they simply Tweet every time they publish a new blog post on their website or a new video to their YouTube channel.

Bottom line: Twitter is a powerful, "short & sweet" social broadcasting platform that can play a very significant and positive role in any business' online marketing strategy.

Advertising on Twitter could be one of the most impactful decisions you make in your business' online marketing strategy. Why? Because of the sheer numbers, for starters. There are well over 300 Million active users on Twitter (nope, not a typo) and that's nothing compared to the total created accounts which is sitting at over 1.3 Billion (yes, with a "b"). Of that gargantuan amount, around half, 550 million, actually ever Tweet and another 500 million visit the site each month to read tweets and news without logging into their accounts. One-third of all US social media users are on Twitter and 80% of active users access the site via mobile. These days, anyone who is anyone is on Twitter, including over 80% of the world's leaders.

So that's all well and good from a purely personal perspective. Clearly the numbers are there. But what about business? Why should you market and advertise there? Well, if it's any indication, 65.8% of US businesses with 100+ employees are marketing on Twitter. 58% of the world's top brands have built and maintained enormous Twitter followings (100K or more).

And how active are all these businesses on Twitter? 92% of them Tweet more than once per day, nearly half of them (42%) Tweet up to 5 times per day, and 20% of them go crazy and Tweet up to 10 times each day. Yeah, there's a good bet that these companies have a very good reason for putting so much marketing energy into Twitter.

So the businesses and companies are clearly on board. But what do consumers think? Well, the average Twitter user follows 5 companies and 80% of them have mentioned a brand or business in a Tweet. 54% of consumers on Twitter reported that they have taken action in response to seeing brands mentioned in Tweets (e.g. Retweeting, going to the brand's website, searching for the brand, etc). To finally drive the point home, Twitter revealed in 2016 that total paid ad engagements had grown a whopping 208% year-on-year. Yikes.

LinkedIn

LinkedIn isn't just for helping you recruit top talent or finding your dream job. It's a powerful means of organic B2B marketing. You can of course leverage paid marketing on LinkedIn, but even with paid marketing every business needs to invest in building their organic presence. Just as with other social media platforms, LinkedIn is a global site—which is an effective means of growing your business well beyond your local service area. While B2B marketing is the most effective, don't discount LinkedIn for B2C.

LinkedIn is a site dedicated to professionals so the mindset when joining, posting, searching, and networking is quite unique when compared to Facebook or Twitter. While the site may not be as saturated, that is something you can use to your advantage. Users join and log in for professional purposes, meaning you have a built-in captive audience. Just take a look at some of the stats.

There are over 467 million users in over 200 countries around the world. The US has the largest number of users, followed by India, Brazil, Great Britain, and Canada. LinkedIn is available in over 24 languages. There are 1.5 million professional LinkedIn Groups in hundreds of industries. 57% of users are male and 44% are female. 41% of millionaires use LinkedIn. 13% of users are between the ages of 15 and 34—including over 40 million students and recent college grads. 94% of online marketers use LinkedIn to distribute content. 71% of professionals believe LinkedIn is a credible source for professional content. 80% of B2B leads come from LinkedIn. 46% of B2B social media traffic comes from LinkedIn. So obviously, LinkedIn is the perfect place to market your business.

Instagram

Instagram is a powerful photo sharing app. When it comes to leveraging this social platform for business, it's all about visualizing your brand. While you can certainly post photos to any and all of your other social platforms, Instagram differentiates itself (even from Pinterest) with filters which empower absolutely anyone to turn their photos into engaging and brand-building works of art. When it comes to deciding which social platforms to add to your website, and post to regularly—Instagram certainly can't be ignored.

One of the most noteworthy differences between Instagram and some of the other sites you might be considering for your brand or business, is that Instagram is a mobile app. While you can head to Instagram.com after you have created an account and perform limited functions, the majority of the functions must be used within the app. Downloading the app is free for both Android and Apple. If you are using Instagram for your business, set up your Facebook account first. Even if you are not yet active on Facebook, you will need to link your Instagram account to its parent company (Facebook) to transition it from a regular account to a business account.

We know that you only have so much time in the day, so you might be in search of some quantifiable facts as to why Instagram is where you should be investing your time and resources. Here are some statistics that businesses across every industry simply can't ignore. Instagram has over 700 million active users (yup, you heard that right), 400 million of whom use the app every single day. 80% of these users are outside of the U.S. Over 80% of Instagram users follow and engage with multiple businesses, products, or services. Over 250 million Instagram users engage with the Instagram stories (paid advertising) each day which makes it a dream come true if paid ads are your focus. Users share over 95 million photos and videos each day. Most Instagrammers are between 18 to 29 years old. 38% of women use Instagram and 26% of men. Over 8 million registered businesses use Instagram. Over 120 million Instagrammers engage with brands directly after their Instagram engagement—visit their website or profile URL, direct message in Instagram, email, call, visit other social platforms, or get directions. By the end of 2017, 70% of brands will be on Instagram. Over 60% of users have learned about a new product, services, business, or brand after finding them on Instagram. Instagram posts with hashtags receive over 12% more likes, comments, tags, and shares. The average business or brand posts 5 times per week.

So, clearly Instagram is where you should be marketing, based on audience size, usage and engagement, and demographics – not to mention that every other business is marketing there, which should tell you something.

Pinterest

There are so many social media platforms to choose from, that most business owners focus their time and attention on one or two. When deciding which sites are the best to brand and market your business, you must not forget the visually engaging Pins and Boards found on Pinterest.

There are a few standout ways in which Pinterest varies from other social media sites. While you can "follow" users, and they can "follow" you—it's not about friends and followers. Instead, it is about generating instant access to engaging visual imagery and informative Pins regarding any and every area of interest. These Pins can then be added to a user's personal boards for future reference. Anyone can access any other users Pins by the category or keywords related to the Pin. While each Pin can have a bit of text or even a URL, the goal is not the "here's where I am or what I'm doing" topic of most social media platforms. Instead, a relevant comment regarding the post, and what it represents is standard. Most importantly, unlike Facebook and Twitter where your posts peak engagement is rarely more than 5 days (or a few hours) Pins can continue to show up in search results indefinitely.

If you're inclined to stick with the major players, like Facebook and Twitter, don't write off Pinterest until you take a closer look at the statistics. First off, let's talk about the shear size of your potential audience. Pinterest boasts an insane 150 million active users. Yeah, you heard that right. 70 million of those are in the US, with 80 million outside the US. As can be expected, Pinterest activity is proportionately astronomical. There are over 75 billion Pins, which have been posted to over 1 billion public and private user boards. Over 2 billion shopping pins are posted daily. 87% of users make purchases after seeing products or services on Pinterest and 93% use it with an eventual purchase (online or offline) as their primary goal, which makes Pinterest a no-brainer platform for those seeking to sell goods and services to a shopping-minded audience. And 72% of users make offline purchasing decisions based on Pinterest content. So it's not just a goldmine for online businesses.

The average Pinterest user session is just over 14 minutes, which is very impressive when you compare that to most other social media platforms. 14 million rich pin articles are posted every day and a whopping 5% of all web traffic comes from Pinterest. 80% of Pinterest users access the site from a mobile device, so mobile marketing and mobile-friendly content is very important here, and 2 out of 3 pins are posted by businesses or brands, so you've got some competition. Oh, and if you happen to be in the culinary niche, guess what: there are over 1.7 billion recipes on Pinterest.

As for your audience make-up, 81 percent of Pinterest users are women, so the "Pinterest is for girls" stereotype clearly has some truth to it, at least from a market research perspective. But don't worry, if your target audience is males, the percentage of men on the site is increasing rapidly, making up about 40% of new users recently. In case you were wondering, the most popular categories for these new male Pinterest users are technology, food and drink (big surprise, right?). As for age, millennials are using Pinterest just as much as Instagram. The median age of users is 40 years old, but the most active "pinners" are under the age of 40.

So, now that we've established that social media is an absolute must-have marketing channel for your business, it's time to establish some social marketing goals, which we'll do in the next section.

Chapter 2:
Social Marketing Goals

Establishing marketing goals is critical to the success of your social marketing. Countless entrepreneurs and businesses have setup a social presence, made a few posts, and then let it sit untouched for months or even years. This is usually due to a lack or absence of goals. So, before you even begin establishing any sort of social presence or strategy, you need to establish clear marketing goals.

Your goals should be specific, measurable, and attainable. They can be long term, short term, or a mix of both. Deadlines and milestones can be helpful as well. "I want to increase my social following" would be an example of a bad goal that will likely result in your marketing efforts petering out after a while because there are no specific milestones. "I want to gain 1,000 likes by Christmas" is an example of a good goal. It's specific, measurable, and certainly attainable. Below are some examples of the various goal categories you might be interested in.

Traffic to Website (Sales, Leads, Content)

Probably one of the most popular goals of Social Marketing is to funnel your traffic back to your own web properties. After all, most businesses don't to business "on" social media, per se. You're leveraging social media to obtain traffic and convert that social traffic into brand-followers, leads, prospects, and customers. So maybe your goal is to get people to a landing page with a free offer where they can subscribe to your list and become a lead. Maybe they're being sent to a sales page or an eCommerces store. Maybe you just want to do some content marketing and send them to your blog. Whatever the case, the end goal for a lot of businesses will likely be bringing social traffic AWAY from social platforms and over to their own web properties.

Social Following

In this goal category, your aim is to build a large number of followers. This usually means "likes or followers" in the case of a business/brand page or it could mean "friends" if you're focusing on your personal profile. The main sought-after benefit here is to increase the number of people who will see your posts or tweets in their feeds. In this sense, your social posts become similar to sending out email broadcasts via your autoresponder. It should be noted that some social networks have recently adjusted their algorithms in such a way that people tend to see less posts from businesses they've followed. This means a much smaller percentage of your followers will see your posts in their feeds today than did in the past. Still, if you grow a large enough community, this can still be very beneficial and if your content is engaging enough to get a lot of traction in the form of likes, comments, and shares, you can significantly increase the range of your organic reach into people's feeds.

Passive Presence

Some businesses might have purely passive goals. Simply being present and discoverable inside social platforms is a benefit that has wider appeal and greater utility than you may think. In many cases, a company's social presence might supersede or even totally replace what was once the role of a website or blog. Your business' phone number, address, directions, hours of operation, mission statement and so on can often be put on your social accounts and, depending on your audience, that might be where most people seek you out, rather than your website. The ease of posting announcements, updates, photos, and other content without relying on a web developer or having to use a web-building platform also makes social presence an attractive alternative to the traditional website model. This same approach can also be used for events, communities, and brands.

Brand Awareness

Another goal that's less thought about might be spreading brand awareness and recognition. If you're just starting out, there's a good chance your brand might be in need of a jumpstart. If nobody's ever heard of you, a great way to increase recognition is to simply create and share unique, helpful, or entertaining content and get your name, logo, and overall brand identity in front of as many people as possible as many times as possible. If this is your goal, you want to avoid being salesy in the beginning. Ensure you're focused almost entirely on posting helpful, relevant, or entertaining content.

Expand Existing Audiences

If you've already got an audience, your goal might be to make it bigger. This can be done via several social marketing methods. Sharing viral content, either curated or created yourself, can lead to a huge increase in your social audience. Recently, a restaurant in Southern California released a 60 second video with shots of people enjoying their signature menu item, an enormous T-bone steak topped with melted cheese, and it went viral in one day. They had already garnered a respectable audience prior to the video, but after the video, their Facebook audience and engagement skyrocketed (and so did their foot traffic). Although creating your own viral content like that can be great, if you don't have the time or means to do so, you can simply leverage existing content that's already proven itself to be viral by curating/re-sharing it with your own comments or angle added to it. Also, a few humorous images and memes can't hurt either.

Other ways to expand existing audiences can include contests, sweepstakes, and gamification. Assuming your offers/prizes are compelling enough, incentivized sharing can be very effective. Just ensure your methods are permitted by each social platform's Terms of Service.

Enhancing or Repairing Public Relations

Do you want to set your company apart in the public eye? Do you want to associate your brand with feelings of good will and community involvement? Did you accidentally spill a ton of crude oil into the Gulf of Mexico and kill a bunch of fish? If any of these apply to you, then enhancing or repairing public relations could certainly be a good social marketing goal for your business.

You can bet that when a certain major energy giant had an oil spill on its hands a few years ago and became public enemy number one, they went into PR repair overdrive. They were literally hated by almost everybody and their business could easily have disappeared off the face of the earth. But instead, they handled it masterfully and began pouring millions, if not billions, of dollars into massive PR campaigns to improve their image and highlight their commitment not only to fixing the mess, but to the environment in general. This PR campaign lasted years and you can bet they leveraged social media platforms like Facebook as well.

But it doesn't take a humiliating public catastrophe to make PR enhancement a good idea. This is a goal that any business can engage in. Non-sales related campaigns can include photos or videos that foster positive values and goodwill or even involvement in social movements (be careful not alienate half your prospects) and noble causes. Did your business recently donate to a charity, build a school in a third world country, serve food at a local pantry? These are all things to post about. These don't necessarily need to be about things that your business participated in. They can be content about general things like a heart-warming video about helping the poor or caring for the elderly. Special holidays like Christmas, Thanksgiving, or Mother's Day also present opportunities to leverage emotions, foster goodwill, and enhance your PR.

Market Research

A hugely beneficial goal of social marketing is market research. If you're just starting your business or going down a new path, social media can be an excellent place to learn more about your audience and your market. This can be done in a structured way with things like surveys and questionnaires, or in a less structured way by simply engaging with your audience, commenting, asking questions, and so on. Also, lurking or conversing in social groups related to your industry can teach you a ton about what your customers want and who they are. Beyond that, you can monitor your competitors' pages and groups to see what their customers like and what they're complaining about so you can adjust your business accordingly. Creating your own group and engaging within it is another great way to get a constant stream of market/audience data flowing into your business. Ultimately, your goal should be to come up with one or two ideal customer avatars that you can then base your marketing and product development on.

All of the goals you've learned about in this section require some sort of overall social strategy. So that's what we'll be covering next.

Chapter 3:
Content Strategy

Now that you've got your goals established, it's time to start cranking out some quality marketing content. Let's look at some of the types of content you can create, curate, and leverage in your social marketing.

Basic Posts

So much emphasis has been placed on visual media like photos, memes, and videos in recent years that many people have forgotten the power of good old-fashioned text. A basic textual post can accomplish a lot and, in fact, can actually stand out a lot today in people's feeds that are often filled with non-stop cliché viral images and videos. A standard textual post can be an excellent pattern interrupt in these cases. A textual post, whether it be from your personal profile, a business page, or a group, can be about anything you want. It might be a piece of content in and of itself, like an informative blog post. It could be a link back to some other content elsewhere such as your blog or website or your

Youtube channel. Other great ideas for content are questions, stories, and jokes. These can be great for boosting engagement and getting conversations started.

Also, a poll is a great way to boost engagement in your textual posts as well. Asking questions is already something that boosts engagement and people love voting on things, so naturally when you pair the two together you're likely to get some great social traction. HINT: For polls, always say something like "tell us 'why' in the comments below" so people can talk about their opinions and get some conversations and extra engagement going.

Image Posts and Memes

It's been almost a decade, and we're STILL seeing images Boromir from Lord of the Rings looking at us in our newsfeeds and telling us about how "One does not simply... [insert funny variable here]". Why? Because it gets people's attention, gets your point across, and usually still results in a few likes, shares, or comments. Whether it's Sean Bean saying "One does not simply run Facebook ads without a using a tracking pixel" or the Dos Equis guy sipping on a beer and saying "I don't usually try to lose 5 pounds in one week, but when I do, I use High Intensity Interval Training", the fact is memes work in almost any niche. In fact, it's precisely their goofy and ironic application to unexpected niches that causes them to be so funny and get a rise out of people. So, it's settled, if you can find a few minutes per week to make a funny meme for your niche, it's definitely worth your time.

Other images can be beneficial as well. If you're working an "authority" angle, try posting images of you on stage at events. If you're promoting a free report or free digital offer, you can use an image of the eCover itself or even a generic stock image Adobe Stock. Make sure the images are relevant to your offer and audience. So, if you're targeting restaurant owners, a smiling business owner standing outside of their restaurant might work. If you're doing a weight loss product, a stock photo of a woman stretching or a man running might be the ticket. If you're selling physical products, use an image of the product itself or of a person using the product. And remember, these are organic posts, not paid ads, so you're not bound by some of the usual restrictions like the "text to image" space ratio and so on (although there are still some ToS that apply to all content, so be sure to familiarize yourself with those).

Videos

Video. The uncontested king of engaging content. This still hasn't changed. In fact, if anything, it's becoming even more of a norm than ever. If you're not using videos in your social marketing, you're missing out big time. While it used to be common to use YouTube for hosting your videos and simply embed/link to them on other social platforms, many platforms like Facebook and Twitter have since then started to beef up their own video hosting functionality. For example, today,

Facebook is giving YouTube a run for its money and many people are now beginning to lean toward using Facebook as their primary video sharing venue. This is beneficial not only to Facebook, but also to marketers because Facebook has made its videos super engaging by making them autoplay, with no sound, while people are scrolling/swiping past them in their newsfeeds. This results in a ton of views and engagement. This same trend is being seen on other platforms as well.

So, video content is a must. But what types of videos should you incorporate into your marketing? There are several options. Regular vlogs, talking head videos, selfie videos, screen capture videos, instructions, tutorials, tips & tricks, funny videos, motivational videos, animated explainer videos, short "ad" videos, inspirational videos, slideshow videos... the list goes on and on. Anyway, you're able to convey content or messages via videos is great. More recently, some social sites like Facebook have introduced live streaming videos. You can literally host a live video feed or a show and even invite others on for split-screen interviews/discussions from just about any device.

Curated and Repurposed Content

Not all content needs to be created by you or your team from scratch. One very popular form of content marketing is content curation. This means finding existing content from someone else and simply re-sharing it yourself. This can be done simply by using the Share button to share other interesting or entertaining posts and adding your own comment or commentary.

Another way to curate content is to manually republish it. This can mean copying excerpts from someone's blog, a news article, a book, and so on. Just ensure you always attribute it to the author (e.g. "Here's some great tips from the folks at [blog name]") and try to always put your own comments at the beginning or end and/or ask your audience for their thoughts on it. This is a mutually beneficial form of content marketing because you're spreading the exposure of the other entity's brand name (which they'll appreciate) while also posting content with almost no work required on your part.

Another option for quick content publishing is to repurpose your existing content. Do you have ebooks, reports, or guides of your own? Why not take a chapter from one of your ebooks, tweak the beginning and end a bit, and publish it as a Facebook post? Heck, you could turn an ebook or report into a whole series of social posts covering a whole week. Have a blog on your website with interesting articles and posts? Why not post a teaser/excerpt from each blog post (old or new) and a link to the post in question? Same goes for videos, podcasts, interviews, and so on. If you've been online long enough, there's a good chance you'll be able to repurpose a lot of content into social posts.

Content Planning

Planning out your marketing strategy is super important. The last thing you want is for your social presence to turn into one of those where you set up an account, post a few things and then becomes lifeless for months at a time (this happens a lot). When people see this, you instantly lose credibility. That's why it's important for you or your team to have a robust content posting schedule and strategy. Ideally, you should be posting almost every day at least. However, this need not always be content designed from scratch. Instead, you can set aside two days of the week that are for original created-from-scratch posts or videos, while all the days in between only require a re-shared post from elsewhere or a quick meme/image. Set aside another day of each week for a video post and maybe another day for a community poll. If you have a regularly updated blog or YouTube channel, you can also simply add a new step to your blog posting or YouTube uploading workflow in which after each post or upload, a link should to the new content should be shared/teased via social channels. There are a number of ways to easily incorporate daily social posting into your weekly routine. It would also be a good idea to establish a daily or at least weekly routine for you or a team member to go through all your posts and reply/interact with your audience if they commented or asked questions.

Tools, Services, and Help

Maintaining a regular and active social presence can be a little difficult if your business is already busy as it is. If it becomes too overwhelming for you there are several options for lightening the load or at least making it easier to manage. Firstly, there are tools like HootSuite and OnlyWire that make social media posting, scheduling, and planning much easier. If you'd like to have your content created for you, there are a handful of paid third-party services out there that will literally create and post content for you on a daily basis. $99 Dollar Social would be one example of this. You'd simply fill out a profile of what type of content you want and what industry/niche you're in and let them take care of the rest. Finally, it might be worth it to hire a new team member specifically to handle your social media marketing (or delegate the responsibility to an existing team member who has time available to do it). This individual would be in charge of posting, commenting, replying, moderating, and so on.

So, social marketing is clearly an incredibly valuable, and arguably critical part of any online business today. As you've learned in this guide, it can be a lot easier to establish a social marketing strategy and routine than you may have previously thought. But none of it will count for anything if you don't start applying what you've learned right away. To that end, start implementing the steps of the following battle plan today.

Battle Plan

Step 1: Determine your social marketing goals.

Step 2: Determine what type of social platforms/presence best fits your business.

Step 3: Draft up a content plan with your team.

Step 4: (Optional) Consider using tools or services to lighten the load.

www.ingramcontent.com/pod-product-compliance
Lightning Source LLC
Chambersburg PA
CBHW071444210326
41597CB00020B/3934